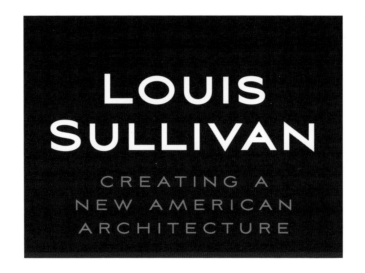

LOUIS SULLIVAN

CREATING A NEW AMERICAN ARCHITECTURE

PATRICK F. CANNON

PHOTOGRAPHY BY

JAMES CAULFIELD

Pomegranate

SAN FRANCISCO

Published by Pomegranate Communications, Inc.
Box 808022, Petaluma, CA 94975
800 227 1428 | www.pomegranate.com

Pomegranate Europe Ltd.
Unit 1, Heathcote Business Centre, Hurlbutt Road
Warwick, Warwickshire CV34 6TD, UK
[+44] 0 1926 430111 | sales@pomeurope.co.uk

Front cover: A view of the lobby staircase landing at the Guaranty Building (Buffalo, New York, 1895).

Back cover: The Schlesinger & Mayer department store complex (Chicago, 1899–1903).

Library of Congress Cataloging-in-Publication Data
Cannon, Patrick F.
  Louis Sullivan : creating a new American architecture / by Patrick F. Cannon ; photography by James Caulfield.
      p. cm.
  Includes bibliographical references and index.
  ISBN 978-0-7649-5771-0 (hardcover)
 1. Sullivan, Louis H., 1856-1924—Criticism and interpretation. 2. Architecture—Illinois—Chicago Region.
 3. Chicago (Ill.)—Buildings, structures, etc. I. Sullivan, Louis H., 1856-1924. II. Caulfield, James. III. Title.

  NA737.S9C36 2011
  720.92—dc22

                                        2010036753

Pomegranate Catalog No. A192

Designed by Lynn Bell, Monroe Street Studios, Santa Rosa, California

Printed in China
20 19 18 17 16 15 14 13 12 11   10 9 8 7 6 5 4 3 2 1

Contents

PREFACE

Photographer James Caulfield and I undertook to produce this book at the behest of Thomas F. Burke, president of Pomegranate Communications, Inc. He felt that a fresh look at Louis Sullivan's Chicago work was needed, and we enthusiastically agreed.

Having lived in the Chicago area for most of my life, I was familiar with Louis Sullivan and his work. For my interest in Sullivan and Chicago architecture generally, I have to thank the late Carl W. Condit, whose course on the Chicago school I took when I was a student at Northwestern University. His landmark work on the subject is listed in the bibliography.

Most of what I knew about Sullivan came from Professor Condit's course and book and through my study of Frank Lloyd Wright and the Prairie school, the subjects generally of our three previous books. Sullivan figures prominently in biographies and studies of Wright, who worked for Sullivan for five years and who later described him as his "Lieber Meister," or "beloved master."

The more intensive reading and study required for this book revealed a man who reached the peak of his profession before he was forty and then suffered a long decline that ended with his death, in near poverty, at age sixty-seven. Even before his death, the Chicago practice of tearing down the old to make way for the new and more profitable had taken several of his designs. In the years that followed, many more would be demolished, including major buildings such as the Chicago Stock Exchange and the Schiller Building; indeed, of the nearly two hundred Sullivan designs that were fully or partially built, fewer than forty still stand.

Every structure in Chicago designed by Sullivan that is still standing and not changed beyond recognition was photographed for this book. Even the burnt-out shell of the Kehilath Anshe Ma'ariv (KAM) Synagogue, the home of Pilgrim Baptist Church at the time of the fire in 2006, is included. To add perspective, we have included selected buildings outside Chicago. Originally we had not intended to do this, but we realized that nothing remained in Chicago that Sullivan designed after 1905 except the façade he designed for the Krause Music Store in 1922. His one Prairie period home in the Chicago area, the Henry Babson House of 1907, was gone, as were his best tall buildings, the Chicago Stock Exchange and the Schiller Building. Of the small banks that constituted most of his practice after 1905, none was built in the Chicago area.

To be sure, black-and-white historical photographs of most of the demolished Sullivan-designed buildings of Chicago are available, and we have included many of them in this book. We preferred not to repeat the sad word "demolished" in the captions for those buildings, so unless it is otherwise noted you can assume that the buildings illustrated with black-and-white historical photographs are gone. And although black-and-white photographs may actually work best for some modern buildings, they do not work at all well for an architect for whom color was a critical element of his aesthetic.

Although we might have chosen other buildings, those we did travel outside Chicago to photograph—the Guaranty Building in Buffalo, New York; the Wainwright Building in St. Louis, Missouri; the Peoples Federal Savings and Loan Association in Sidney, Ohio, and other small banks; and the Harold C. Bradley House in Madison, Wisconsin—are all in good original or restored condition and thus reflect the architect at his best and most representative.

This book is not meant to be a biography, but we include a brief biography that may help the reader understand how Sullivan's upbringing and education influenced his work, and we provide additional biographical material in describing the genesis and creation of individual buildings. Those interested in a thorough treatment of Sullivan's life should seek out Robert C. Twombly's *Louis Sullivan: His Life and Work,* which is listed in the bibliography. I have also relied upon Professor Twombly's book to date Sullivan's buildings.

Finally, Sullivan's accomplishments were intimately associated with the considerable abilities of Dankmar Adler, his longtime partner, as an architect and structural engineer and, perhaps of equal importance, a generator of commissions. Adler's many connections in Chicago's Jewish community led to numerous residential and commercial commissions for Adler and Sullivan, including synagogues and Chicago's most prominent Jewish men's club. Sullivan even designed Adler's house. It should be noted that the firm Adler & Sullivan came into being only in May 1883; prior to that it was known as Dankmar Adler, Architect.

Louis Henry Sullivan, c. 1920, in a portrait believed to be by Frank Werner. Courtesy Ryerson and Burnham Libraries, Art Institute of Chicago.

Acknowledgments

I have many people to thank. Tim Samuelson, cultural historian for the City of Chicago and expert on (and lover of) the work of Louis Sullivan, provided guidance on the surviving works of Adler & Sullivan and those of Sullivan alone after the partnership dissolved. He also answered the many questions that arise in researching a work of this kind. He knows the landmarks of Chicago, and he is one himself. At Roosevelt University, James Caulfield and I were assisted by Tom Karow, Julie Sumner-Garibaldi, and Calvin Harris. Jennifer Turner and Steve Sell helped us photograph the magnificent spaces of the Auditorium Theatre. While we worked on the book, the Sullivan Center, formerly the Carson Pirie Scott department store, was undergoing restoration and renovation. For keeping us informed about its progress, we are grateful to Doug Gilbert, Bob Score, and Gunny Harboe of Harboe Architects, the firm responsible. For assistance in photographing the Art Institute of Chicago's Sullivan fragment collection, and the recreated Chicago Stock Exchange Trading Room it houses, we are grateful to Erin Hogan and Chai Lee. At the Institute's Ryerson and Burnham Libraries, where I obtained many of the historical photographs in this book, I was helped by Danielle Kramer and Mary Woolever. Similar services were provided by Bryan McDaniel of the Chicago History Museum and Adele Barbato of the Bostonian Society. My son, Patrick, searched for and downloaded the images I needed from the Historic American Buildings Survey. At the Charnley-Persky House, headquarters of the Society of Architectural Historians, access and cooperation were provided by executive director Pauline Saliga and the building's manager, Heather Plaza-Manning. Adler & Sullivan's Guaranty Building in Buffalo, New York, is owned and lovingly maintained by the Hodgson Russ law firm; Paul Pellegrino and Gary Schober made it possible to include their magnificent building in this book. Another Sullivan building that has been lovingly maintained is the Peoples Federal Savings and Loan Association in Sidney, Ohio; our thanks go to Douglas Stewart, the company's president. Likewise, we are indebted to the Grinnell Area Chamber of Commerce, current occupant of the Merchants National Bank building; and to John Pratt at the Farmers & Merchants Union Bank. Sullivan built only two private homes after 1900. Just one, the Harold C. Bradley House in Madison, Wisconsin, survives. It is now the home of the Sigma Phi fraternity at the University of Wisconsin, and member Andrew Goldemberg helped us gain access. As always, my wife, Jeanette, read and made helpful comments on the text, as did my daughter, Elizabeth. If any errors managed to creep in despite the best efforts of those who helped me, they are entirely my responsibility. Finally, my admiration for my photographer partner, Jim Caulfield, increases with each book we publish. His images do full justice to the great buildings of a truly great architect.

A LIFE IN ARCHITECTURE

*L*ouis Henry Sullivan was born in Boston on September 3, 1856, to Patrick and Andrienne Sullivan. In his curious autobiography, written when he was sixty-six, Louis was strangely dismissive of his father, ascribing little merit to him other than the undoubted fact that he was a self-made man.

Patrick was born in Ireland and apparently learned and practiced his trade as a dancing master in London before immigrating to Boston in 1847. His son tells a possibly fanciful story of Patrick being separated from his father at a fair in Ireland at the age of twelve, not being able to find him again, and thereafter wandering Ireland as an itinerant violinist. According to his son, after Patrick learned his adult trade in London, he perfected it in Paris at the feet of the leading French masters.

Unlike the majority of Irish immigrants in 1847, Patrick traveled to the United States not to escape the effects of the potato blight and famine but to advance in his trade in a country where his Irishness might be less of a hindrance than it might have been in class-conscious England.

Something should perhaps be said about just what a "dance master" was at that time. It wasn't like a teacher at today's Arthur Murray or similar studio, which essentially teaches adults how not to embarrass themselves at weddings and dinner dances. While there would have been some of that, dancing masters mostly taught young people the dancing and social skills they would need in a far busier formal social scene than exists today. During the social season they would routinely attend debuts, balls, and cotillions and would be expected to do their share of dancing.

About the age of twelve . . . this . . . boy, to his own surprise, became aware that he had become interested in buildings: and over one building in particular he began to rave . . . It stood at the northeast corner of Tremont and Boylston Streets. It was a Masonic Temple built of brown granite, light gray in tone and joyous of aspect.

LOUIS H. SULLIVAN
*The Autobiography
of an Idea*

Sullivan in his early forties.
Courtesy Ryerson and Burnham
Libraries, Art Institute of
Chicago.

Sullivan's mother was born Andrienne List in Geneva, Switzerland, in 1835. Her father, Henri, was German; her mother, Anna, Swiss and French. After business reverses in Geneva, the Lists, whose family was reasonably prosperous, were given sufficient funds to reestablish themselves in America. They arrived in Boston in 1850. How Patrick and Andrienne met is not known, but Patrick was attracted to her musical ability—she was an accomplished pianist—and the couple were married on August 14, 1852. He was then thirty-four, she only seventeen.

They had two sons. Albert Walter was born on September 17, 1854. Louis Henry—his middle name probably a tribute to his grandfather—was born two years later, on September 3.

Louis's unhappiness with his father may have been related to Patrick's seemingly endless search for a better place to practice his profession. Over the years, the family moved to New York City, back to Boston, then to Newburyport, Massachusetts, and even out of the country to Halifax, Nova Scotia, before finally moving to Chicago in 1868. Between these various excursions, the Sullivans often stayed with the Lists at their small farm in South Reading,

Massachusetts. Although Louis was still only twelve, it was decided that he would stay with his grandparents and finish his schooling in Boston before rejoining the family in Chicago.

Both Patrick and Andrienne could draw competently and enjoyed sketching during family outings in the countryside, so Sullivan's artistic abilities came naturally. Although most of his drawings that survive are of architectural ornament, those of people and landscapes suggest that he might well have succeeded as a painter had he not chosen architecture. He later wrote that his love of nature was heightened by the years spent wandering around his grandparents' farm and the surrounding countryside.

In his autobiography, Sullivan also tells of walking the streets of Boston, admiring its many impressive buildings and dreaming of becoming an architect. One building he particularly admired was Merrill G. Wheelock's Masonic Temple, a neo-Gothic building whose exuberance appealed to the young man's imagination.

He was in a great hurry to make his dream come true. It would be hard to imagine a more driven young man. While he managed to graduate from grammar school (Rice, Boston, 1870), that would be the last time he graduated from anything. He attended Boston English High

As a young boy, Sullivan liked to walk the streets of Boston, studying its impressive buildings. One he particularly admired was Merrill G. Wheelock's Masonic Temple of 1867. Its eclectic Gothic Revival design appealed to him more than did the very common Classical Revival structures then in fashion. Courtesy Bostonian Society, Old State House Museum.

School, which, although not as famous as Boston Latin, did have a more rigorous curriculum than most high schools of today. After two years and at sixteen years old, he was accepted as a special third-year student at the Massachusetts Institute of Technology.

Founded in 1861, MIT had soon gained a reputation for excellence in engineering and the sciences. In 1868 a school of architecture was added, the first in the United States. Its initial four students had grown to twenty-seven by the time Sullivan arrived in 1872. The school was headed by William R. Ware, a Harvard University graduate who had trained as an architect at a Boston firm before moving to New York to work for Richard Morris Hunt, an acknowledged leader of the profession whose legacy includes George Vanderbilt's Biltmore Estate in Asheville, North Carolina, America's largest private home. Like Hunt, Ware was an exponent of French architectural ideas, so the curriculum was also based on the École model.

In 1873, after only one year, Sullivan decided he had learned all he needed to at MIT, so he went to New York to visit Hunt—perhaps with an introduction from Ware—to seek his advice or (more hopefully) a job. This was not possible, but Hunt did suggest that the young man go to Philadelphia to seek employment with Furness & Hewitt. Frank Furness had been one of the many young architects who worked in Hunt's office. Sullivan's grandfather and uncle lived in Philadelphia, which added to his attraction to the city and provided him a place to stay.

Top: Frank Furness was Sullivan's first architectural employer. The colorful and flamboyant Pennsylvania Academy of the Fine Arts in Philadelphia reflected his personality. Courtesy Historic American Buildings Survey.

Bottom: Main Hall at the Pennsylvania Academy of the Fine Arts. Like Furness, Sullivan would use his considerable talent to lavishly decorate the interiors of his buildings. Courtesy Historic American Buildings Survey.

It turned out that Frank Furness was just the kind of architect who would appeal to young Sullivan, still only seventeen years old. His eclectic and exuberant designs—which matched his larger-than-life personality—were as far from the classicism taught at MIT as they could be. While the Panic of 1873, and the attendant loss of business, cut short Sullivan's tenure at Furness & Hewitt and forced him to join his family in Chicago, he learned a great deal of the practical workings of an architectural practice while there. Although it can't be known what commissions he might have worked on, Furness's colorful and unique Pennsylvania Academy of the Fine Arts would have been one of the possibilities.

CHICAGO—AT LONG LAST (BUT NOT FOR LONG)

In his autobiography, written when he was in his sixties, Sullivan described his reaction when he first saw a city still rebuilding and reinventing itself after the famous 1871 fire had largely destroyed its center:

> The train neared the city; it broke into the city; it plowed its way through miles of shanties disheartening and dirty gray. It reached its terminal at an open shed. Louis tramped the platform, stopped, looked toward the city, ruins around him; looked at the sky; and as one alone, stamped his foot, raised his hand and cried in full voice: *This is the place for me!*

He arrived the day before Thanksgiving. After enjoying Thanksgiving dinner with his parents and his brother, Albert—working as a machinist for the Illinois Central Railroad, whose Chicago to New Orleans division he would one day head—Sullivan spent some time exploring the city before looking for work. What he saw must have astounded him, for Chicago was not only rebuilding but also in the midst of raising its grade so that proper sewers could be installed to help alleviate chronic outbreaks of waterborne disease.

Unlike the situation in Philadelphia, opportunities abounded for young architects in Chicago. Sullivan wrote later that he walked the city to find a building he admired and then looked up its architect. The building he admired was the Portland Block; its architect was Major William Le Baron Jenney. A product of Phillips Exeter Academy and Harvard's Lawrence Scientific School (like Sullivan's MIT teacher William Ware), Jenney had completed his engineering education at the École Centrale des Arts et Manufactures in Paris in 1856. After service in the Civil War, he eventually made his way to Chicago and opened an architectural practice in 1869.

His young employee later commented that Jenney "was not an architect except by courtesy of terms. His true profession was that of engineer." Jenney is known today primarily for developing the steel framing techniques that led to the skyscraper, of which his Home Insurance Building of 1885 is considered by many to be the first. In addition to Sullivan, many of the young architects who would be associated with the Chicago school passed through

Jenney's office, including William A. Holabird, Martin Roche (the two would become partners), Irving K. Pond, Howard Van Doren Shaw, and John Edelmann.

It was Edelmann who sponsored Sullivan's membership in the Lotus Club, a group of amateur athletes who met weekly at a site on the Calumet River, some fifteen miles south of the city. Sullivan's brother, Albert, also became a member. Club members competed with one another in swimming, running, rowing, and other sports and also competed as a team with similar clubs.

It isn't known what Sullivan worked on in Jenney's office, but it's likely that he continued to develop his drafting and tracing skills. He wrote very little about his work there, but his autobiography makes clear his enjoyment of the physical exercise and camaraderie of the Lotus Club. His membership was, however, to be interrupted, for in July 1874, after less than eight months' time in Chicago, he left for New York to take ship to England, with Paris and the École des Beaux-Arts as his ultimate destination.

EUROPEAN INTERLUDE

Paris had been on Sullivan's mind for some time. His father had lived there as a young man. His mother's family spoke French and had extolled the virtues of Paris to him. At MIT the architectural program was based upon École principles, and Parisian Eugène Létang had been William Ware's closest associate there. Jenney had been trained in Paris, as had Richard Morris Hunt, the first American to attend the École.

Before he boarded the *Britannic* for the ten-day passage to Liverpool, Sullivan visited Hunt's office and talked to Sidney Stratton, who gave him valuable advice on what he would need to do in Paris. Upon arrival in England, he took a train and spent approximately two weeks in London, enjoying the city's architecture while being somewhat repelled by its pockets of poverty and the coldness of shopkeepers and others he met.

Early in August he set out for Paris, along the way seeing Rouen Cathedral, with which he was suitably impressed. He eventually found lodgings at 17, rue Racine in the Latin Quarter, conveniently located near the École.

William Le Baron Jenney's Home Insurance Building (Chicago, 1885) is considered by some to be the first skyscraper. Sullivan didn't consider his employer to be a true architect, but his innovations in steel framing would enable Adler & Sullivan to create some of the most notable early tall buildings. Courtesy Ryerson and Burnham Libraries, Art Institute of Chicago.

Since the École then had only thirty places available for new architectural students, entrance was by competitive exam. Sullivan would have to improve his French and prepare in other subjects. He would also need a sponsor and letters of recommendation. In this, his MIT and Hunt connections were probably critical. He found a sponsor in Emile Vaudremer, who had been Létang's instructor, and he may have had letters of introduction from him and from Hunt and Stratton.

In addition to mathematics and other related subjects, the test included preparing a plan, section, and elevation for an assigned building. This had to be done in twelve hours, with the results judged the next day. Many aspirants failed the test once or never passed. Unlike Henry Hobson Richardson, who failed in his first try, Sullivan passed. He was only eighteen years old, but he was a young man in a hurry.

Sullivan spent just ten months in Europe. In addition to his lectures and studio work at the École, he traveled to Rome, at that time a place of pilgrimage for architecture students and budding artists. In addition to the usual monuments, he was particularly impressed by the works of Michelangelo, whose Sistine Chapel he saw as the work of "a great free spirit" and the "first mighty man of Courage." Michelangelo's approach—melding painting, sculpture, and architecture to create a coherent and powerful visual whole—would inform Sullivan's own vision to the end of his life.

CHICAGO AGAIN—AND FOREVER

With an architectural education that largely stressed classicism, Sullivan—still only eighteen—returned to Chicago to begin a career that would lead him to create a more purely American architecture.

He moved in with his parents and brother and reestablished his relationships with the Lotus Club and his friend John Edelmann, who not only gave him work but also became his intellectual mentor and companion. He began to read more widely: art histories by Hippolyte Taine and other Europeans and works by the Americans Bret Harte, Mark Twain, and James Russell Lowell.

For Edelmann's firm, Johnson & Edelmann, Sullivan participated in two commissions. In 1876 he executed interior frescoes for the Chicago Avenue church of the famous evangelist Dwight Moody and did similar work for the Sinai Synagogue. On the latter, Burling & Adler acted as associated architects, thus beginning a relationship between Dankmar Adler and Louis Sullivan that would last for nearly twenty years. Accounts of Sullivan's work in the local papers were highly complimentary, but no photographs or illustrations of the frescoes are known to exist.

Edelmann left Chicago later in 1876 to seek the commission for a large cathedral in Cleveland. Although he later returned, after trying his hand at horse ranching, his close relationship with Sullivan had largely ended.

Sullivan probably began working with Dankmar Adler on a freelance basis in 1879, after he had set up shop as "Louis Sullivan, Designer." He became a partner in Adler & Company in mid-1881 and a principal in Adler & Sullivan on May 1, 1883. Before the partnership was dissolved in 1895, the firm had received approximately 180 commissions. Of these, 60 were residences, 33 were commercial or office buildings, 27 were manufacturing facilities, 17 were theaters of various kinds, and 11 were warehouses. The rest were a mix that included hotels, railroad stations, synagogues, churches, and even tombs. By any measure, Adler and Sullivan were among the leaders of the profession in Chicago.

Dankmar Adler was twelve years Sullivan's senior. He was born in 1844 in Stadt Lengsfeld, in the German state of Saxe-Weimar-Eisenach. His father, a rabbi and cantor, moved his family to Detroit in 1854 and became chief rabbi of Temple Beth El. During the family's time in Detroit, his son developed an interest in architecture and served an apprenticeship in the office of E. Willard Smith. In 1861 Adler's father accepted a position in Chicago with the Kehilath Anshe Ma'ariv (KAM) Synagogue. Young Adler found work with the architect and engineer Augustus Bauer, but the Civil War intervened and Adler enlisted on his birthday in 1862.

Adler saw a great deal of action and was wounded. He spent the last nine months of his service with the US Corps of Topographical Engineers, which substantially broadened his professional knowledge. When the war was over, he returned to Bauer's office. After working there and in other offices, he formed his own firm in 1871 with Edward Burling. Burling was later charged with malpractice. He was acquitted, but when the promoters of the Central Music Hall were uneasy about him and offered the commission to Adler alone in 1879, Adler dissolved the partnership.

The widely held assumption that Adler wasn't an architect at all, but essentially a talented engineer and acoustician, is wrong. Prior to Sullivan's joining the firm, and probably even for some time after, Adler would have been largely responsible for designing the buildings credited to both Burling & Adler and Adler & Company. While not works of genius, the designs were competently done and compared favorably with the work of other Chicago firms of the time.

The Borden Block (foreground; Chicago, 1880) was designed by Adler & Company after Sullivan joined the firm but prior to his being made a partner. While Sullivan may have had a hand in the building's decorative elements, its basic design is almost certainly Adler's. Looming behind it is Adler & Sullivan's Schiller Building, designed just ten years later. Courtesy Ryerson and Burnham Libraries, Art Institute of Chicago.

Because he soon recognized Sullivan's developing genius for design, Adler eventually and very sensibly left it to him, while concentrating on the increasingly complex engineering demands of the firm's ever larger and more complex commissions.

While Sullivan was certainly not antisocial, Adler seems to have been mostly responsible for getting clients and keeping them happy. Although he didn't have many close friends, Sullivan was widely acquainted and belonged to several clubs, including the prestigious Chicago Club. But he could be quite opinionated, particularly about his work. This was not a major issue so long as he had Adler as a buffer, but it became much more of a problem when the partnership dissolved.

Adler's Jewish background was also a major advantage for the firm, whose client list included dozens of Jewish names; many were members of his father's congregation. The firm also got commissions for synagogues and the Standard Club, at that time an exclusively Jewish institution.

The firm's prosperity in the 1880s and early 1890s permitted club memberships for its principals as well as a new vacation home for Sullivan, who otherwise seemed content to live in apartment hotels. His friends Helen and James Charnley introduced him to Ocean Springs, Mississippi, on the Gulf of Mexico a few miles from Biloxi (soon after, Adler & Sullivan would design the Charnleys' now famous Chicago house). By the winter of 1890–1891 he had built a cottage on the eleven acres of land he had purchased. He fell in love with his retreat and for the next twenty years spent as much time there during the winter as he could, constantly expanding his beloved gardens. The house, unfortunately, was destroyed in 2005 by Hurricane Katrina.

Sullivan's brother, Albert, also bought land in Ocean Springs but never built a cottage, being content to park his private railroad car on a nearby spur. He was by then general superintendent for the division of the Illinois Central Railroad that ran from Chicago to New Orleans. The brothers seemed to have had a close relationship until Albert married Mary Spellman in 1893. Louis was living with

Sullivan's cottage at Ocean Springs, Mississippi, provided both a refuge from Chicago's harsh winters and an opportunity to enjoy the natural world he loved so much. Courtesy Ryerson and Burnham Libraries, Art Institute of Chicago.

Sullivan on the steps of the cottage, c. 1900. Courtesy Ryerson and Burnham Libraries, Art Institute of Chicago.

them in a house he designed, but he was apparently asked to leave when Mary had a daughter in 1896. While the details are not known, it appears Louis took this hard and became estranged from his brother, an estrangement that would last for the rest of his life.

The year before, Sullivan had also lost his partner. Business had dried up after the Panic of 1893, and Adler felt he must take a job to support his family. Sullivan, who had no family to support, took this personally and, later, when conditions improved, would refuse to reestablish the partnership.

Another loss came in 1893 when an argument over a loan led to Frank Lloyd Wright's departure. The loan in question had been made by the firm to Wright in 1889 to enable him to build his home in Oak Park. The $5,000 loan having been repaid, Wright asked for the deed, which apparently Sullivan refused to give him. They argued, and Wright either quit (his version) or was fired. Not open to question is that Wright was Sullivan's most talented assistant.

Fortunately, Sullivan's dwindling staff after 1895 included George Grant Elmslie, who remained faithfully with Sullivan until the lack of commissions forced him to leave in 1909. He then formed a partnership with William Gray Purcell. Their firm would go on to produce Prairie-style buildings second in number only to Wright's.

After 1895 Sullivan's most important client was the Schlesinger & Mayer department store (later Carson Pirie Scott). Between 1896, when he altered existing buildings on State Street, and 1903, when he did the same on Wabash Avenue, his work for the company was almost continuous. Included was the flagship store at State and Madison streets, an icon of retail design and one of the architect's masterpieces.

The reasonable income of those years permitted Sullivan to marry in 1899. Sullivan's sexual orientation has been questioned by some biographers, perhaps because of his participation in the Lotus Club and other men's clubs and his long bachelorhood (he was forty-two when he married). There is absolutely no evidence to support this. What is certain is that he married Margaret (born Mary Azona) Hattabaugh on July 1.

Little is known about Margaret or the details of their meeting and relationship. She was twenty on her wedding day. The decline of their marriage mirrored the decline in Sullivan's fortunes. Between 1903 and 1909 he completed just five buildings. Not only was Sullivan

Margaret Sullivan at the time of her marriage to Louis. Courtesy Ryerson and Burnham Libraries, Art Institute of Chicago.

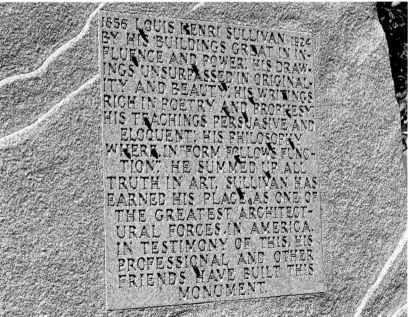

increasingly depressed, but he also seems to have been drinking heavily, a fault that according to some had plagued him for most of his life. These and other factors—including moving to cheaper and cheaper apartments as his fortunes declined—can't have been pleasant for a young woman. Margaret left him in 1909, although she did not divorce him until 1916.

Ironically, the few commissions that Sullivan received after 1909—mostly small-town banks—have come to be widely admired. They were not enough to support him, even when supplemented by his continued writing. He came to depend more and more on the generosity of his friends, including Frank Lloyd Wright, with whom he had reconciled, and Adler's son Sidney. His written pleas to them and others make painful reading, coming as they did from a man who had been widely recognized as one of America's greatest architects. His last years were spent working to finish his autobiography (*The Autobiography of an Idea*) and *A System of Architectural Ornament, According with a Philosophy of Man's Powers,* whose drawings had been commissioned by the Burnham Library at the Art Institute of Chicago. Both were published by the Press of the American Institute of Architects. At the urging of his friends, copies were rushed to Sullivan, arriving on April 11, 1924, three days before he died at the age of sixty-seven. He died penniless. His debts and funeral expenses were paid by his friends, who also paid for the headstone that marks his grave and expresses their respect for him.

Top: Sullivan's friends took up a collection to pay for his headstone at Chicago's Graceland Cemetery, where Sullivan's parents are also buried and where the tombs he designed for Martin Ryerson and Carrie Eliza Getty draw thousands of visitors every year. The spelling of Sullivan's middle name used here ("Henri") is a common mistake.

Bottom: The rear of the headstone contains a heartfelt tribute from Sullivan's friends and fellow architects.

Housing a Growing Chicago

. . . I insist strenuously, that a building should live with intense, if quiescent life, because it is sprung from the life of its architect.

LOUIS H. SULLIVAN
*Kindergarten Chats
and Other Writings*

Frank Lloyd Wright gave the impression in his autobiography that Louis Sullivan turned over residential commissions to him because he wasn't interested in them. Like much of what Wright wrote about his early career, it was self-serving and somewhat misleading. While Wright may (the word is used advisedly) have indeed been given wide latitude to design residences such as the famous James Charnley House, it was probably more because Sullivan was busy with major commissions and simply couldn't do all the work himself.

In fact, prior to Wright's joining the firm, Adler & Sullivan designed more houses and other residential buildings (nearly sixty) than any other type. With the success of the Auditorium Building, the firm did not seek them as aggressively, since the partners believed, correctly, that more important commissions could be had.

In Professor Robert Twombly's biography of Sullivan, an apartment block and residence for John Borden in 1880 are listed as Sullivan's first residential designs. These and the great majority of the architect's residences have subsequently been demolished. Indeed, of the nearly sixty single-family and multiple-unit residences that Sullivan designed, fewer than ten remain standing today, including his last built residence, the 1909 Harold C. Bradley House in Madison, Wisconsin.

One reason so many have been lost is simply their location. Many of Adler & Sullivan's clients in the 1880s were Jewish people whom Dankmar Adler knew through his religious and social networks. Because Jews were then excluded from many North Side and near–South Side neighborhoods, they built their homes farther south, from roughly 30th to 60th streets, from Lake Michigan on the east to what is now Cottage Grove Avenue on the west. With the exception of parts of the Kenwood and Hyde Park neighborhoods, which retain some of their Jewish identity largely as a result of efforts of the nearby University of Chicago to stabilize the area in the 1960s, large sections deteriorated and were eventually demolished to make way for new housing, expressways, and other developments. Much was still vacant in the early years of the twenty-first century.

The John Borden House (Chicago, 1880) was one of Adler & Sullivan's largest residential commissions. It later led to a commission for the downtown Borden Block of office buildings. Photograph courtesy Chicago History Museum.

With a few exceptions, most of Adler & Sullivan's residences were what would now be called town or row houses, separated from their next-door neighbors by little more than a party wall or a narrow gangway; Sullivan would have had to design only the front and rear façades. While his designs were mostly tasteful and even pleasing, they did not stand out from the work of other architects who designed housing.

The James Charnley House of 1891, shown in some detail on these pages, was a departure from what went before, just as the Wainwright Building in St. Louis signaled a new and higher level of accomplishment in office building design for Adler & Sullivan. It is a pity, then, that in the last thirty years of his career Sullivan was able to design only two more residences, the 1907 Henry Babson House in Riverside, Illinois, later demolished, and the surviving 1909 Harold C. Bradley House in Madison, Wisconsin.

The Halsted dining room retains its original carved wood fireplace, ceiling and window trim, and floor.

Opposite: The Ann Halsted House (1883) is a large freestanding residence in Chicago's Lincoln Park neighborhood.

A view of the main staircase, hall, and side door.

A strongly vertical art glass window provides light for the landing between the first and second floors. The floors and trim are original. Door transoms could be opened to provide air circulation.

The living room fireplace includes leaf, shell, and fan motifs that are more traditional than Sullivan's later, more inventive decorations. Notice the fan finials, which are used on the exteriors on some of Sullivan's early designs.

This view from the living room to the front hall shows the original art glass panes on the inside doors, as well as the pocket doors, which still function with very little effort.

An interesting feature of the south-facing windows in the living room and library (these are in the library) is shutters that can be folded into and hidden by the window casework.

A closer view of the first two units (south to north) shows the differing treatments of the front windows and entry doors. The brackets below the second-floor sills are, however, uniform across the entire façade.

Opposite: Adler & Sullivan designed these row houses for Ann Halsted in 1884 (Lincoln Park, Chicago). Four were built at first, with the fifth added the next year. The first, third, and fifth have identical façades, as do the second and fourth.

In the same Lincoln Park neighborhood as the two Halsteds, the Leon Mannheimer House (1884) has a large bay that helped bring maximum light into a building that was crowded close to its neighbors and built before electric lighting was widely available. The front entrance had been "modernized" when the current owner, an architect, bought the building. Lacking plans or a contemporary photograph, he studied other period Sullivan buildings when designing what we see in this photograph.

Adler & Sullivan's narrower town houses typically had the main staircase facing the front door.

To make maximum use of available space, storage was often provided under the stairs.

This view into the bay shows the large west-facing windows. The fireplace (left) is not original, but its design is based on one from the same period in one of the Halsted row houses.

Detail of exterior decorations on the Leon Mannheimer House, showing fan and shell motifs.

One of two surviving Adler & Sullivan houses on Chicago's South Side, the Joseph Deimel House (1886) has a two-story bay and typical Sullivanesque decoration on the porch pediment and cornice.

Also on the South Side, the Gustaf Eliel House (1886) retains its original arched first-floor window, but it has replacement siding and panes in the oriel window above.

The Albert W. Sullivan House (Chicago, 1891) was ultimately the home of Sullivan's brother and his family. It was originally intended to be a home for the brothers and their mother, but Andrienne Sullivan died before she could move in. It is obvious that Sullivan lavished more than the usual attention on its beautifully detailed design. Photograph by Chicago Architectural Photographing Company, courtesy Ryerson and Burnham Libraries, Art Institute of Chicago.

Wright's William H. Winslow House (1894) in suburban River Forest, Illinois, although designed for a more expansive lot, shares an essential simplicity with the James Charnley House, as well as the same Roman brick and symmetrical façade. Winslow was a supplier of ornamental iron to Adler & Sullivan and most of the major Chicago architects.

Opposite: Frank Lloyd Wright may have designed the James Charnley House (1891) as he claimed, but Sullivan surely supervised his young assistant very closely, given that James and Helen Charnley were close friends of Sullivan; they had introduced him to his beloved Ocean Springs, Mississippi, and were his neighbors there. With its beautifully simple and symmetrical design, the house stood (and still stands) in stunning contrast to its neighbors on Chicago's exclusive Astor Street. Decoration is limited to the very narrow cornices and the porch. The house is now the headquarters of the Society of Architectural Historians and is called the Charnley-Persky House to honor Seymour Persky, who provided the funds that enabled the society to purchase the property.

The entry door of the
James Charnley House
opens onto a foyer
whose steps lead to the
reception area.

A fireplace with a mosaic surround and hearth is flanked by arched openings for the main stairs and storage cabinets. Similar arches are used for all openings on the first floor.

This view is from the dining room. The library is on the opposite side of the reception area.

The fireplace end of the dining room is bay shaped. Ornament is limited to the fireplace surround.

The library also has a fireplace. The bust on the mantel is of Seymour Persky.

Opposite: This view of the main staircase is from one of the small rooms that flank the front door.

The second and third floors feature balconies with a skylight above. The doors at left lead to the porch.

Access to the porch is either from the balcony (shown) or from the master bedroom. The openings in the brickwork at right provide light for the master bedroom closet.

The stairway to the third floor is behind the screen. The balcony railings have intricately detailed fretwork panels.

These stairs lead to the third floor. The screen dissects the view and leads the eye to the skylight, which provides abundant light for the core of the house.

REACHING FOR THE SKY

The epigraph to this chapter is
drawn from Louis H. Sullivan, "The
Tall Office Building Artistically
Considered," *Lippincott's Magazine*
57 (March 1896): 403–409.

Chicago has long laid claim to being the birthplace of the modern skyscraper. While the genesis of the engineering techniques that permitted buildings to rise ever higher is a long one, there seems little doubt that they came together for the first time in the ten-story Home Insurance Building of 1885, designed by William Le Baron Jenney.

Jenney was a trained engineer turned architect. Despite the Home Insurance Building's steel frame and masonry nonbearing curtain wall construction, it was just a taller version of its neighbors. No attempt was made to express its verticality; indeed, it had no fewer than four horizontal bands dividing its façade into five separate units.

Many of Adler & Sullivan's office building designs of that time and earlier weren't unlike the Home Insurance Building. But when the firm began to exploit the new structural possibilities available with steel framing, Sullivan began to think seriously about how best to emphasize the new buildings' most obvious feature—their height.

The late 1880s were busy years for the firm, not least because of the extreme demands of designing and constructing the Auditorium Building, begun in 1886 but not finished until 1889. The Auditorium had an office tower that rose to sixteen stories, but only five floors rose above the main building, which was of masonry load-bearing construction. It was the commission for the Wainwright Building in St. Louis in 1890 that was the turning point in Sullivan's development of a true tall building aesthetic. Frank Lloyd Wright later recalled Sullivan putting a rough sketch of the building on his table and Sullivan's young assistant realizing his master had solved the "problem" of the skyscraper.

How had he done it? While he would not have put it in these terms, he had seen the tall building as a column consisting of a base, shaft, and capital. All of his important tall buildings, except the Chicago Stock Exchange, follow this pattern: a basement for the furnace and other utilities, a two-story base for shops and similar uses, a sill, and then the multistory main office section, with identically expressed bearing columns and nonbearing mullions rising to the attic, often highly decorated and capped by an equally highly decorated cornice. Typically the massive corner piers rise uninterrupted

Far right: The Rothschild Building (Chicago, 1880–1881) was typical of Sullivan's office building designs prior to the advent of steel framing. A premium was put on providing the maximum window size permitted by bearing walls. The building was designed before Sullivan's name was added to the firm of Adler & Company. Photograph by Harold Allen, courtesy Ryerson and Burnham Libraries, Art Institute of Chicago.

Near right: A fragment of the ornamental frieze from the cornice of the Rothschild Building. Collection of the Art Institute of Chicago.

from the sidewalk. Spandrels separating the windows are recessed so that the columns and mullions rise uninterrupted to the cornice.

The two Chicago buildings that best expressed Sullivan's ideas—the Chicago Stock Exchange and the Schiller Building—have both been demolished, the Schiller in 1961 and the Stock Exchange in 1972. Only fragments of these great accomplishments remain in museums and private collections. Tragically, photographer and preservationist Richard Nickel died in an accident while trying to salvage some pieces of the Stock Exchange.

Although the interior is much changed, the Wainwright Building in St. Louis has a largely original exterior. Also in St. Louis, the Union Trust Building of 1893 still stands but with significant changes to the base. Sullivan's only New York City commission, the Bayard (later Bayard-Condict) Building, exists in a largely restored condition, as does the Guaranty Building in Buffalo, New York, perhaps Sullivan's best tall building, restored in the 1980s.

Sullivan's treatment of the façade of the A. F. Troescher Building (Chicago, 1884) was quite restrained, with ornamented spandrels used only between the second and third floors. The ground-floor arches are repeated at the top. Photograph by J. G. Replinger, courtesy Ryerson and Burnham Libraries, Art Institute of Chicago.

The Ryerson Building (Chicago, 1884) is more highly decorated, perhaps the result of a more lavish budget. Both columns and spandrels are decorated. Three of the floors have bay windows, which would have maximized available light. The awnings were fairly common, used in summer to minimize the effect of direct sunlight. Martin Ryerson made his fortune in lumber and was an active real estate developer who provided much work for Adler & Sullivan, eventually including Ryerson's tomb in Graceland Cemetery. Photograph by J. W. Taylor, courtesy Ryerson and Burnham Libraries, Art Institute of Chicago.

The exterior of the Wainwright Building (St. Louis, 1890) looks today much as it did when built (the interior, however, has been significantly changed). The contrast between it and buildings such as the Rothschild and the Ryerson could hardly be more striking. The basic material is red granite, with a slightly darker terra-cotta for the entrance surrounds, spandrels, attic, column capitals, and cornice. While not a "soaring" statement to modern eyes, it was Sullivan's answer to the question of how tall buildings should be expressed.

Opposite: The bold corner columns rise from the ground straight to the highly decorated attic, which has the circular openings the architect often favored.

This pedestrian-level view clearly demonstrates the effectiveness of Sullivan's new tall building aesthetic.

The base of the Wainwright Building is quite plain, with only the entrance surrounds decorated with Sullivan's trademark geometric and foliate designs.

Schiller Building and Garrick Theatre, Chicago

The Schiller Building (Chicago, 1891) combined a theater (later renamed the Garrick Theatre), offices, and club rooms for the German American organization that sponsored its construction. It is as much a testament to Adler's structural genius as it is to Sullivan's design virtuosity. The tower rises to seventeen stories (of which the theater takes seven) and is flanked by two nine-story wings. Behind the tower is a fourteen-story wing, forming the base of a T-shaped plan that ensured outside light would reach every office. Directly to the east (right)—and in strong contrast to it—is Dankmar Adler's Borden Block of 1880. The extent to which Sullivan participated in its design is pure conjecture, but he had joined Adler's firm by then. In this colored postcard image, the gabled building in the distance to the east is Burnham & Root's Masonic Temple Building, at twenty-two stories the tallest building in the world when it was completed in 1892. Postcard published by Acmegraph Company, Chicago, courtesy Patricia A. Sabin.

This view of the top of the Schiller Building's tower is from a 1923 advertisement for the Northwest Terra Cotta Company, Sullivan's supplier on numerous commissions. The vertical columns terminate in arches. Above is an arched colonnade, which is a smaller version of the colonnade at the base of the columns. Decorated spandrels are used only at the top and bottom of the façade. The lantern that tops the tower gives the design an almost Moorish quality. Courtesy Ryerson and Burnham Libraries, Art Institute of Chicago.

Right: This exterior column from the Schiller Building was one of three sited just above the second-floor loggia. Collection of the Art Institute of Chicago.

A contemporary view of the theater shows one of the boxes, with a sculptured relief by Richard Bock illustrating a scene from one of Friedrich Schiller's poems. Photograph by Barnum & Barnum, courtesy Chicago History Museum.

A photograph taken by Richard Nickel before demolition shows that the reliefs and other decorative elements had been removed in what became, at various times, a television studio and movie theater. As in the Auditorium Theatre, the space was defined by a series of arches that diminished in size as they approached the stage. Photograph by Richard Nickel, courtesy Historic American Buildings Survey.

Nickel did his best to document the building before its demolition. This view shows a staircase and elevator lobby that served the offices. Photograph by Richard Nickel, courtesy Historic American Buildings Survey.

Only fragments remain of the Schiller. This is a section of the star-pod design from the theater's proscenium vault. Collection of the Art Institute of Chicago.

This fragment is from the stringcourse on the first-floor loggia. Collection of the Art Institute of Chicago.

Four of the original twelve busts of famous German artistic figures were salvaged from the second-floor loggia and installed on the façade of Chicago's famous Second City improv theater.

While not a tall building, and not expressed as such by Sullivan, the Mayer Building (Chicago, 1892) is one of Adler & Sullivan's purest expressions of structure. It originally had a decorative terra-cotta cornice, which was removed by order of the city when similar ones in Chicago began to deteriorate. Photograph by Cervin Robinson, courtesy Historic American Buildings Survey.

Detail of the Mayer Building's corner column capital. Photograph by Cervin Robinson, courtesy Historic American Buildings Survey.

The Chicago Stock Exchange (1893) achieved its verticality not through uninterrupted columns and mullions but by narrow projecting bays that began at the third-floor sill and ended at the colonnade that ringed the building below the cornice. The LaSalle Street façade had six bays, and the Washington Street façade had three. They alternated with particularly large "Chicago" windows, which consisted of a large, unmovable center light flanked by movable sashes. The Chicago window was used by many of Adler and Sullivan's contemporaries, most particularly William Holabird and Martin Roche. Although local architects and preservationists attempted to save the building, it was demolished in 1972. As mentioned earlier, Richard Nickel—some of whose work appears in this book—died in an accident while trying to salvage some of the building's artifacts. Courtesy Ryerson and Burnham Libraries, Art Institute of Chicago.

MAIN STAIRCASE

THE EXCHANGE

WASHINGTON ST. ENTRANCE

INTERIOR OF THE EXCHANGE

THE CHICAGO STOCK-EXCHANGE.—Drawn by J. Gleeson after Photographs.—[See Page 31.]

A measure of the national interest in Chicago's tall buildings can be seen in this page from the January 12, 1895, issue of *Harper's Weekly*, with drawings by J. Gleeson. Courtesy Ryerson and Burnham Libraries, Art Institute of Chicago.

Through the efforts of Richard Nickel, Tim Samuelson (currently the City of Chicago's official historian), architect John Vinci, and others, some of the fabric of the building was saved. The LaSalle Street entrance was reconstructed on the grounds of the Art Institute of Chicago.

Elevator bank with T-plates from the lobby of the Chicago Stock Exchange. Collection of the Art Institute of Chicago.

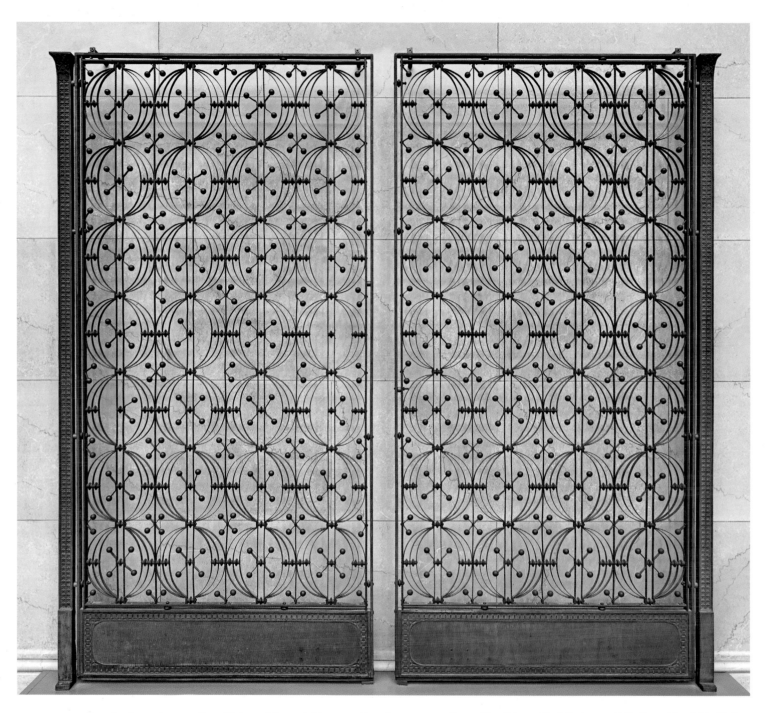

Two elevator enclosure grilles with baseplates and side support bars from an upper floor of the Chicago Stock Exchange. Collection of the Art Institute of Chicago.

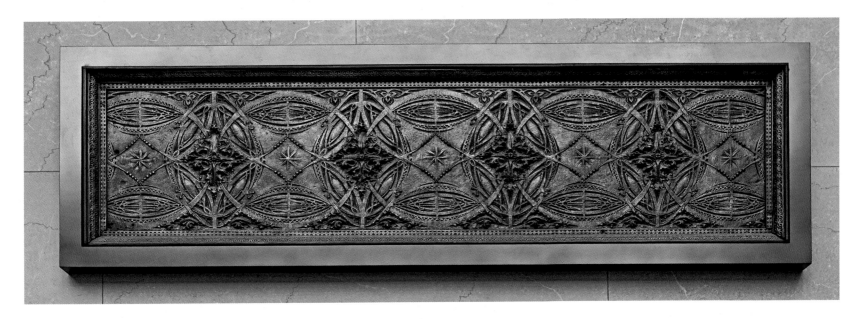

Frieze panel from the elevator assembly in copper-plated cast iron. Collection of the Art Institute of Chicago.

Door kickplate from the Chicago Stock Exchange. Collection of the Art Institute of Chicago.

The ceiling has three massive beams. The stenciling on the beam at left is darker, as it was salvaged from the original trading room and reinstalled during the room's reconstruction.

Opposite: The Stock Exchange trading room was reconstructed in 1976–1977 at the Art Institute of Chicago by the architectural firm Vinci & Kenny. This view shows the entrance doors, podium, and stock quote chalkboards, one each for the New York and Chicago stock exchanges. Virtually every surface in the room is covered with Sullivan-designed decorative stenciling.

As indicated by the large windows on the south and east sides of the reconstructed room, the Stock Exchange would have had abundant natural light. The ceiling skylights were artificially lit.

This view, looking west, shows the visitors' balcony that overlooks the trading floor.

Opposite: The room is supported by four massive columns covered in faux marble and capped by beautifully detailed capitals.

A closer view of the main and balcony columns, beam stenciling, and skylights. The light fixtures feature the small, clear bulbs used so effectively by Sullivan, most notably in the Auditorium Theatre.

The visitors' balcony has its own skylight. Two of the four balcony columns are shown. While the beam they help support is highly decorated, the rest of the balcony has more restrained stenciling.

The Guaranty Building (Buffalo, New York, 1895) was the last commission completed by Adler & Sullivan before the partnership was dissolved. Lack of business caused by the depression that began in 1893 led Adler—who had a family to support—to leave the firm and take a job with the Crane Company, a manufacturer of elevators. The Guaranty Building—perhaps the most richly decorated commercial building in America—later became the Prudential Building, and a major restoration was completed in 1982. Today it is owned by the Hodgson Russ law firm, its main tenant. The firm, which participated in its preservation and restoration, bought it out of bankruptcy in the 1990s and has lovingly maintained it ever since. It is again now known generally as the Guaranty Building.

Every inch of the Guaranty Building, except the glazing, is covered with terra-cotta molding. While the overall conception was Sullivan's, its execution was left largely to George Grant Elmslie, upon whom Sullivan would rely heavily in years to come. Rather than looking fussy, the combination of geometric and foliate designs helps the building soar gracefully from base to top.

Arched forms begin above the entrance
doors and are repeated just below the sill, in
the sill itself, in the spandrels, and in the attic
openings below the cornice.

This corner view shows the circular attic openings topped by arches, as well as the foliate capital that completes the massive corner pier.

The foyer ceiling, with the entrance colonnade at right.

The entrance is at left in this lobby view. The spiral staircase descends to the lower level.

The elevator lobby
makes lavish use of
bronze and mosaic
tile decoration.

A view of the main staircase from the lobby level. Offices now occupy what would have originally been retail spaces.

A circular landing on the main staircase overlooks another part of the lobby. The oval shape used to decorate the stair railings is repeated in the decorative frieze under the ceiling.

A view of the frieze from the landing.

Another view of the landing, this time looking up. Even the stair risers reinforce the decorative motifs.

Each view offers something new.
Here we see railing, ceiling, frieze,
and skylight.

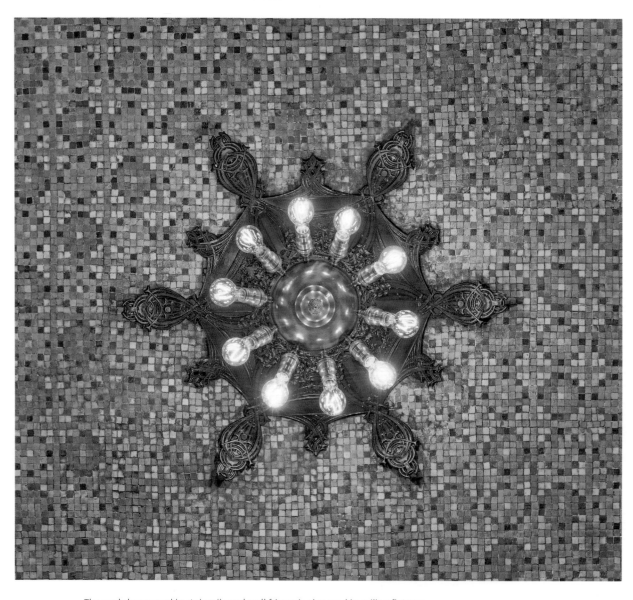

The oval shape used in stair rails and wall friezes is also used in ceiling fixtures.

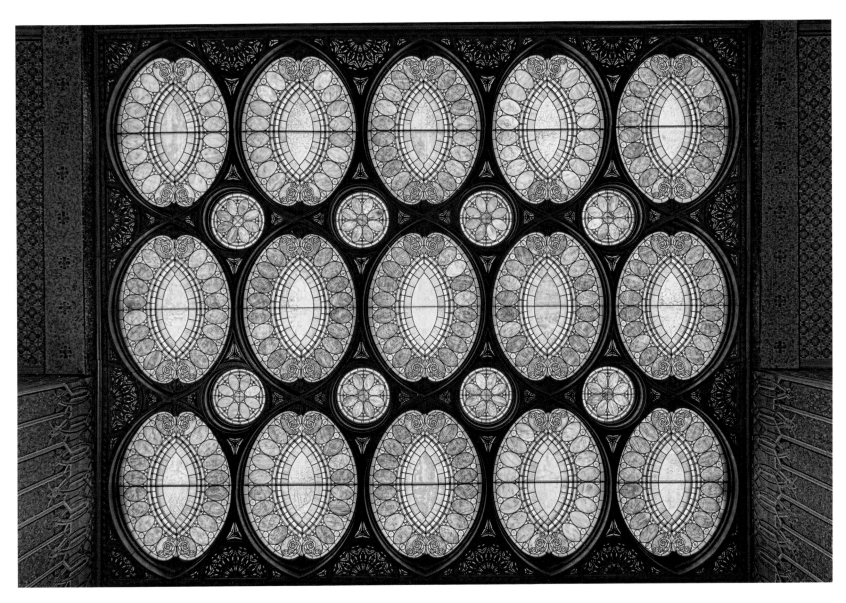

Ovals within ovals and ovals within circles combine for an astonishing lobby skylight.

Left: Even door hardware didn't escape Sullivan's passion for integrated decoration.

Opposite: The Gage Building (Chicago, 1899) was, with the Bayard Building in New York, one of Sullivan's last tall office buildings. It is one of three contiguous buildings—originally of six, seven, and eight stories south to north—whose basic design was by Holabird & Roche. Now directly across Michigan Avenue from Millennium Park, all three were originally meant to house millinery firms. One of these companies, Gage Brothers, wanted something more elaborate for the northernmost building and insisted that Sullivan be hired to do the façade. Four floors were added later, but the basic design remained. While the arrangement of windows remains the same, originally they were topped by Luxfer prisms, glass blocks designed to both amplify and diffuse outside light. Curiously, Frank Lloyd Wright designed prisms and an office building using them (never built) for Luxfer. Compared with that of the Guaranty Building, the decoration of the façade is relatively restrained, but it is certainly typical of Sullivan's tall buildings. The original base was, unfortunately, "modernized" at some stage.

THE WONDER OF THE AGE

We have in us romanticism, and feel a craving to express it. We feel instinctively that our strong, athletic and simple forms will carry with natural ease the raiment of which we dream, and that our buildings thus clad in a garment of poetic imagery . . . will appeal with redoubled power.

LOUIS H. SULLIVAN
*Kindergarten Chats
and Other Writings*

When it was dedicated on December 9, 1889, the Auditorium Building was hailed as the wonder of the age. Not only was it the largest building in the world, but its seventeen-story tower was also the highest structure in Chicago. Its 4,200-seat theater, designed to accommodate the most elaborate operatic productions, was the largest permanent facility of its kind in the world. In addition, the structure included a 400-room hotel and abundant retail space. No wonder, then, that President Benjamin Harrison attended the dedication.

The Auditorium Building was and is one of Adler & Sullivan's grandest accomplishments. But the real hero may have been the man who spearheaded the effort to build it in the first place, Ferdinand W. Peck (1848–1924). Peck, whose father had made a fortune in what had become the fastest-growing city in the world, was an art and music lover who hired Adler & Sullivan in 1885 to renovate the Industrial Exposition Building in order to house the hugely successful Chicago Grand Opera Festival. Its success encouraged Peck to organize the Chicago Auditorium Association the following year.

Despite the festival's success—in a two-week run, 90,000 people attended twelve operas—selling Chicago's movers and shakers on building such a large theater wasn't easy, until Dankmar Adler floated the idea of supporting the opera house with an income-generating hotel, along with office and retail spaces. Mixed-use complexes such as this are common now, but the Auditorium was unique for its time.

The association was formally incorporated in December 1886, and at a meeting presided over by Marshall Field, Peck was elected president. Adler and Louis Sullivan were chosen as architects, despite some misgivings about Sullivan's comparative youthfulness—he was just thirty. Balancing Sullivan's youth was Adler's acknowledged expertise as both a structural engineer and a builder of acoustically successful theaters. The firm had previously designed several theaters, including the McVicker's Theater in Chicago and the theater of the Academy of Music in Kalamazoo, Michigan. Adler's skill in acoustics and the fame of the Auditorium Building would later garner the firm a consulting role in the design of the Metropolitan Opera House in New York.

An interior view of Chicago's Auditorium Theatre, taken from the stage. While it has had its ups and downs as an opera house, the theater, now operated by Roosevelt University, is a popular venue for large-scale musicals, concerts, and ballets.

The Auditorium would be an aesthetic opportunity for Sullivan but a daunting engineering challenge for Adler. It would be not only the largest building in the world but also the heaviest, at just over 100,000 tons. And Adler would have to design a structure within a structure for the theater. While the foundations of large buildings in Chicago would soon consist of caissons drilled to bedrock, the Auditorium is supported by something that resembles a series of rafts floating on the subsoil. The tower, for example, is supported on a raft five feet thick, reinforced with eight layers of timbers, rails, and I-beams. Because of the building's weight, Adler planned for a settlement of no less than eighteen inches.

Sullivan constantly refined his designs, starting with a rather fussy and picturesque design with sloping roof, gables, cupolas, oriels, and other decorative touches. Eventually the design was pared down to the restrained flat-roofed building we see today. Interiors, of course, are another matter altogether.

The final exterior design owes much to the influence of Henry Hobson Richardson, one of America's most admired architects, whose Marshall Field & Company wholesale store of 1887 had a profound effect on Sullivan and other designers. Designed in a style that has come to be known as Richardsonian Romanesque, it had a massive presence and dignity unmatched in Chicago. At the same time, Richardson designed the famous John J. Glessner House, which still stands as a reminder of Richardson's

Top: Henry Hobson Richardson's Marshall Field & Company wholesale store (Chicago) was designed in 1885 and was nearly complete when Sullivan began to finalize his design for the Auditorium Building in 1887. His debt to Richardson, whose untimely death in 1886 robbed America of one of its greatest architects, is clearly apparent. Photograph courtesy Art Institute of Chicago.

Bottom: The Standard Club (Chicago, 1887–1888) was perhaps the first Adler & Sullivan building to exhibit Richardson's influence, with its rusticated limestone facings and simple wall treatment. Photograph by J. W. Taylor, courtesy Art Institute of Chicago.

genius. Sullivan's infatuation with Richardson's work didn't last long, but in addition to the Auditorium, his influence can be seen in the Walker Warehouse, Standard Club, Kehilath Anshe Ma'ariv (KAM) Synagogue, and Pueblo Grand Opera House in Colorado, among other buildings.

While the exterior has its own solid dignity, it is Sullivan's treatment of the interior spaces of the theater and hotel that guaranteed the building's fame. The sheer variety and inventiveness of Sullivan's forms and decorations are unmatched. It is difficult today to imagine assembling the army of artisans and craftsmen that had to be mobilized to execute the architect's elaborate designs. The designs themselves, in their incredible variety, had to progress from Sullivan's hand to final working drawings. For this he had another army of draftsmen, including Frank Lloyd Wright and George Grant Elmslie.

All of this, the complexity of both structure and decoration, resulted in a final cost of approximately $3.4 million, an immense sum for the time. While small profits were made in the early years, financial problems eventually became the norm. For example, one of the main tenants was the Chicago Symphony Orchestra. Its director, Theodore Thomas, thought the Auditorium Theatre too large for orchestral concerts—he claimed that not enough sound returned to the stage—and insisted that a purpose-built auditorium be constructed. He got his way, and in 1904 the orchestra moved into a new Daniel Burnham–designed hall, now called Symphony Center after recent renovations and additions.

Top: The Walker Warehouse (Chicago, 1888) was even closer to Marshall Field's in form, although the stone had a smooth finish. This view shows the building in the final stages of construction. Photograph by J. W. Taylor, courtesy Ryerson and Burnham Libraries, Art Institute of Chicago.

Bottom: This view of the Walker Warehouse, taken just prior to its demolition in 1953, shows the foliate decoration at the base of the main entrance arch. Photograph courtesy Ryerson and Burnham Libraries, Art Institute of Chicago.

Adler and Sullivan designed, remodeled, or consulted on more than ten theaters during their partnership. The popular McVicker's Theater (Chicago) was remodeled in 1885. Photograph by Kaufmann & Fabry, courtesy Chicago History Museum.

Its life as a home for grand opera was also star-crossed. While it did serve as a home for traveling companies such as New York's Metropolitan Opera, local opera companies weren't able to survive. One that did have some success in the 1920s was the Chicago Civic Opera Company, led by utility magnate Samuel Insull, who moved it to what is now the Civic Opera House, designed by Graham, Anderson, Probst & White and completed in 1929. The Great Depression led to the failure of both the opera company and Insull's utility empire.

By 1941 the Auditorium Building was owned by the City of Chicago, which used it as a serviceman's center during World War II. Among its amenities was a bowling alley installed on the theater's stage!

In 1946 the new Roosevelt University negotiated an agreement with the city to take over the building and convert it to classrooms and offices, with the understanding that it would also eventually restore the theater. Clear title was gained only when the city agreed to forgive back taxes for the right to create an arcaded sidewalk on the north portion of the building and theater to enable the widening of Congress Parkway.

Restoration began in earnest in 1956 and continues to this day. Architects involved include Crombie Taylor; Skidmore, Owings & Merrill; Harry Weese & Associates; Danforth, Rockwell, Carow; John Vinci; and Booth Hansen Associates. While the university has believed it necessary to modernize some areas rather than restore them, in general it has done its best to return the complex to its original glory.

The Schiller Theatre (see p. 54) in Chicago was designed with a German American audience in mind. This plaster relief by Richard Bock depicts the poet Friedrich Schiller, a hero of German culture, riding Pegasus. He is being led by Genius, who carries a torch of enlightenment. Hercules and Diana are shown in the spandrels. The auditorium seated 1,270, less than one-third of the Auditorium Theatre's capacity. Photograph by Barnum & Barnum, courtesy Chicago History Museum.

The Auditorium Building, now the home of Roosevelt University and the Auditorium Theatre, was the largest building in the world when completed in 1889. Its location on South Michigan Avenue, across from Grant Park, gives it a commanding presence. The second-floor loggia was originally open.

When Congress Parkway was widened, part of the first floor had to make way for the current arcaded sidewalk.

The main Michigan Avenue entrance to what was once the hotel is enclosed in an arch very similar to that in the Walker Warehouse. Arches are the dominant feature of the façade.

A grand staircase leads from the lobby to the second-floor lounge. The mosaic portraits on the landing are of Franklin and Eleanor Roosevelt.

Opposite: The main hotel entrance from the inside. The door surrounds are real marble, while the columns in the foreground have faux marble finishes.

Right: A detail of the lobby ceiling shows one of many column capital designs Sullivan lavished on the interior, as well as the decorative stenciling and plaster that are such a feature of the building.

The grand staircase rises a full three stories.

The top of the staircase is lit by a skylight and art glass windows. The stairs in the foreground originally would have led to the first sleeping room level, now classrooms and offices for the university.

The Ladies' Parlor, in the second floor's southeast corner, was restored in 1958 and is now called the Sullivan Room. Its decor is decidedly feminine.

The handsome hotel bar was lost when Congress Parkway was widened and the pedestrian arcade created. Photograph by J. W. Taylor, courtesy Ryerson and Burnham Libraries, Art Institute of Chicago.

This fragment is a section of the hotel bar. Collection of the Art Institute of Chicago.

The main hotel dining room, now the Roosevelt University Library, was at the top of the building. The skylights originally had art glass panes. There are two murals by Albert Fleury. The one on the south end shows a bird-hunting scene, and opposite is a fishing scene; both were presumably related to the hotel menu.

This art glass panel was removed from the dining room ceiling.

The dining room had two alcoves; this is at the south end. The north alcove now contains library stacks.

Now a performance space named Ganz Hall (after the noted pianist and educator Rudolph Ganz, who was for many years associated with Roosevelt's music school), this was formerly a banquet room used primarily for private events. A musician's gallery was just above the location of the current stage. The arched clerestory windows admit natural light, although it is sometimes blocked at certain times of day by the building's mass. The murals, with such subjects as fishing, wine making, and wheat farming, are by Albert Fleury, who was also responsible for the murals in the Auditorium Theatre. Photographed from the entrance door, this somewhat distorted view gives a good sense of the total space.

Sullivan designed twenty column capitals for the room, each of a unique design. They were carved by Robert W. Bates.

Elaborately gilded electroliers hang where the ceiling beams meet. Their exposed incandescent bulbs produce a magical effect in the evening and nighttime hours, the primary times when the room would have been used.

The main lobby of the Auditorium Theatre has art glass windows above the entrance doors. The arched entries begin a journey through a series of arches that culminates in the grand arches of the theater itself.

Two of the grand staircases that lead to the upper lobby. Sullivan designed sections of the tile floor to resemble oriental rugs.

The same fixtures, with exposed clear bulbs, were used on the walls and ceilings in the lobby area. The Auditorium Building was a showcase for emerging electrical lighting systems. In addition, the theater had an air-cooling system consisting of blocks of ice and large blowers.

Cloakrooms were placed between the doors to the Auditorium Theatre's orchestra level.

This view from the landing looks down to the main lobby and up to the mezzanine level.

This view, looking up from the mezzanine level, reveals the decorative stenciling on the landing. The sheer variety of decoration is astonishing.

A low oak railing once separated this fireplace inglenook from the mezzanine foyer.

A view from the balcony toward the stage.

Sullivan designed numerous columns and decorative capitals for every part of the building. These columns support an upper balcony and have capitals that seem to grow organically into brackets.

The theater ceiling originally had a skylight composed of ninety-six windows; twelve were of this design. As with much of the decoration, they were executed under the direction of interior decorators George Healy and Louis Millet, who collaborated with Adler and Sullivan on many commissions.

Albert Fleury created two large murals at the balcony level. This one is called *Spring Song*.

TEMPLES TO GOD, TEMPLES OF COMMERCE

ankmar Adler and Louis Sullivan had what we would now call a general practice. Although perhaps best known for their theaters and tall office buildings, they also received commissions for stores, factories, churches, synagogues, and even mausoleums. After the practice dissolved, in 1895, Sullivan continued to gain similar commissions, adding small banks as his practice began to decline after 1902. Sullivan's last design was for a terra-cotta front for the small Krause Music Store on North Lincoln Avenue in Chicago, a far cry from the extensive work he had done in the late nineteenth and early twentieth centuries for the Schlesinger & Mayer department store in Chicago's Loop.

In the late nineteenth century, Chicago was the fastest-growing city in the world. Between the Chicago Fire of 1871 and the 1929 stock market collapse, which led to the Great Depression of the 1930s, building in Chicago was (with the exception of the usual periodic recessions) substantial and almost continuous. Housing was a large part of this as the population swelled and the city expanded to its current borders. Adler & Sullivan had its share in this, as we have seen.

The firm also had its share of the manufacturing plants that rose on the city's Near North, West, and South sides, conveniently adjacent to railroad tracks and the Chicago River. Many of these multistory factories still stand, although quite a few have been converted to other uses, including loft housing. Many more have been lost as land near the central business district has been found desirable for new high-rise and town house developments.

The new residential areas required commercial centers to serve them. These included not only smaller versions of downtown merchants but also neighborhood department stores and the usual banks, groceries, butchers, druggists, restaurants, and shoe stores. Many of the buildings had retail establishments on the ground floor, with offices or flats above. The more important centers had multistory office buildings (in most cases, elaborately clad in terra-cotta) to provide space for doctors, dentists, lawyers, and other professionals. But the tallest structures in most neighborhoods would have been, and still are, church spires. Many of these churches were built to serve immigrant communities, with services conducted in Polish, Italian, German, Greek, and many other languages.

The Eli B. Felsenthal Store and Flats building (Chicago) was one of only two commissions that Sullivan received in 1906. Its cubelike form, with a flat roof and projecting cornice, relates it to Sullivan's small-town banks, almost the only buildings he would complete in his remaining years. Photograph by Henry Fuermann, courtesy Ryerson and Burnham Libraries, Art Institute of Chicago.

The Kaufmann Store and Flats building (1883) has survived in one of Chicago's most desirable neighborhoods, on one of its most vibrant thoroughfares, North Lincoln Avenue. Its exterior is virtually intact.

Rare survivors: entries to one of the Kaufmann's retail spaces and the upstairs apartments (2312). The plaque denotes the Chicago Landmark status the building was granted in 1996.

Now known as the Jewelers' Building—it was originally designed for Martin Ryerson and leased to wholesale paper merchant S. A. Maxwell in 1882—this is one of several buildings on Chicago's Wabash Avenue that cater to retail and wholesale jewelers. The Loop's elevated tracks run down the middle of Wabash, giving the street its unique ambience.

Across Wabash Avenue from the Jewelers' Building are two Sullivan-designed storefronts that were uncovered in 2008 during restoration of the original Schlesinger & Mayer department store complex. While his design for the main store at State and Madison streets is more familiar, Sullivan was also asked to remodel the fronts of 18 South Wabash (1896) and 22 South Wabash (1903). The department store was eventually sold to Carson Pirie Scott & Company, which recently sold the building and closed the store. The building has been redeveloped for mixed uses. In honor of its architect, the entire complex is now known as the Sullivan Center.

Opposite: The main Schlesinger & Mayer store (Chicago) was built in stages beginning in 1899. The last three bays to the south (right) were added as late as 1961, designed by Holabird & Root to match Sullivan's design. The original cornice had been removed but was rebuilt as part of the building's conversion from a department store to mixed use: retail below and offices above.

Right: The stunning corner entrance pavilion and other ornamental ironwork on the base were designed by George Grant Elmslie, by then fully in command of Sullivan's decorative ideas and technique. According to Elmslie, Sullivan was entirely responsible for the rest of the building. Restoration of the ironwork was completed in 2010.

Display windows are meant to draw customers into a store. It's difficult to imagine any framed more stunningly than these.

This view of the cornice is on the Madison Street side. The soffits are highly decorated, as are the window surrounds, in contrast to the flat faces of the columns and spandrels. To provide maximum natural light to the selling floors, Sullivan designed very large "Chicago" windows, consisting of a fixed central light flanked by movable sashes.

Most of the Schlesinger & Mayer's interior flourishes have been lost to modernizations over the years. These photographs from a page in a 1902 publication of the Chicago Architectural Sketch Club shows some of what has been lost. Courtesy Ryerson and Burnham Libraries, Art Institute of Chicago.

Detail of the main stairway on an upper floor. Photograph by Richard Nickel, courtesy Historic American Buildings Survey.

Detail of the column capital visible in the background of the photograph at right. Photograph by Richard Nickel, courtesy Historic American Buildings Survey.

This view captures the intricacy of the entrance pavilion ironwork. Photograph by Richard Nickel, courtesy Historic American Building Survey.

A circular medallion from a first-floor elevator grille. Collection of the Art Institute of Chicago.

These are examples of interior columns and decorative wooden screens. Note the mosaic tile floor, a Sullivan trademark. Courtesy Ryerson and Burnham Libraries, Art Institute of Chicago.

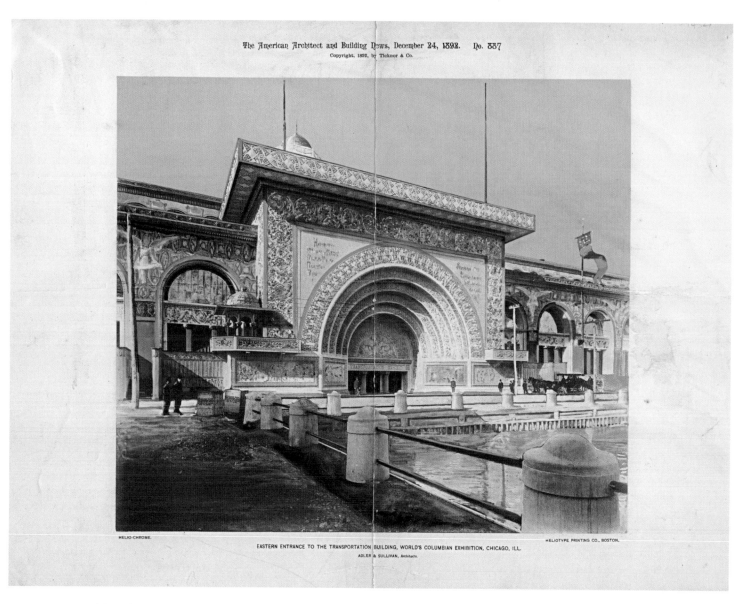

Daniel Burnham was responsible for choosing the architects for Chicago's World's Columbian Exposition of 1893. Most, including Richard Morris Hunt and McKim, Mead & White, were from the East and produced classically styled buildings that together came to be called the "White City." Sullivan's abhorrence of this reliance on past styles was well known. When Adler & Sullivan was given responsibility for the Transportation Building, Sullivan produced an astonishing polychromatic rebuke to the establishment. This color rendering shows the famous "Golden Door." Postcard by Ticknor & Company, courtesy Ryerson and Burnham Libraries, Art Institute of Chicago.

Burnham may have permitted Sullivan's divergence from the fair's classicism because the building was sited away from the famous "Court of Honor," whose uniform whiteness gave the fair its nickname. "The damage wrought by the World's Fair," Sullivan wrote, "will last for a half century from its date, if not longer." Basically a huge train shed, Sullivan's building is, like many of his, a lesson in the use of arches. In addition to those of the "Golden Door," there are no fewer than twenty-six arched windows on the main (lagoon) façade and many more arched clerestory windows above, all meant to provide abundant light for the exhibits within. Photograph by C. C. Arnold, courtesy Ryerson and Burnham Libraries, Art Institute of Chicago.

In addition to the later and larger Standard Club, Adler & Sullivan designed the more modest West Chicago Club (1886) on Chicago's Near West Side. Courtesy Chicago History Museum.

Still occupied by a paint company, the Euston and Company Linseed Oil Plant (Chicago, 1899) has hipped roofs reminiscent of Prairie-style forms.

Now used as a warehouse by the nearby University of Illinois at Chicago, the Standard Elevator Factory (1891) has had most of its windows bricked up, but it's not hard to imagine its original transparency.

Wolf, Sayer & Heller was a meatpacking firm, and Adler & Sullivan designed this addition to the company's Near West Side facility in 1893. Frank Lloyd Wright was still with Adler & Sullivan when the addition was designed and may have been more than usually involved, since he was later commissioned by one of the firm's partners, Isidore Heller, to design a house for his family in Chicago's Hyde Park neighborhood (1896).

Adler & Sullivan's Kehilath Anshe Ma'ariv (KAM) Synagogue (Chicago, 1889) is now a burnt out shell after a fire in 2006, the same year the firm's Wirt Dexter Building (1887) was also lost to a fire. KAM had been occupied for many years by Pilgrim Baptist Church, the legendary birthplace of modern gospel music. Whether it can ever be rebuilt is questionable.

The front façade of KAM is supported by scaffolding. Some of Sullivan's decorative elements survived the fire.

The synagogue's relationship to the contemporary Auditorium Building, Standard Club, and Walker Warehouse, and to Henry Hobson Richardson's Romanesque forms, is clear. Dankmar Adler's father was its rabbi. Photograph by Harold Allen, courtesy Historic American Buildings Survey.

Left: Natural light entered the sanctuary at every level. Decoration was, as one would expect, lavish. Here, as with the Auditorium and Schiller theaters, is a symphony of arches. Photograph by Chicago Architectural Photographing Company, courtesy Ryerson and Burnham Libraries, Art Institute of Chicago.

Opposite, top left: One of the clerestory windows at the balcony level. Photograph by Harold Allen, courtesy Historic American Buildings Survey.

Opposite, top right: The frieze that anchored the ceiling arches featured the Star of David in the center of each foliate panel. Photograph by Harold Allen, courtesy Historic American Buildings Survey.

Opposite, bottom left: This was the sanctuary after it became Pilgrim Baptist Church. Most of Sullivan's decorative flourishes remained, joined by Christian iconography. Photograph by Harold Allen, courtesy Historic American Buildings Survey.

Opposite, bottom right: These art glass windows were at the main level. The column capital was similar in design to the capitals in Ganz Hall at Roosevelt University. Photograph by Harold Allen, courtesy Historic American Buildings Survey.

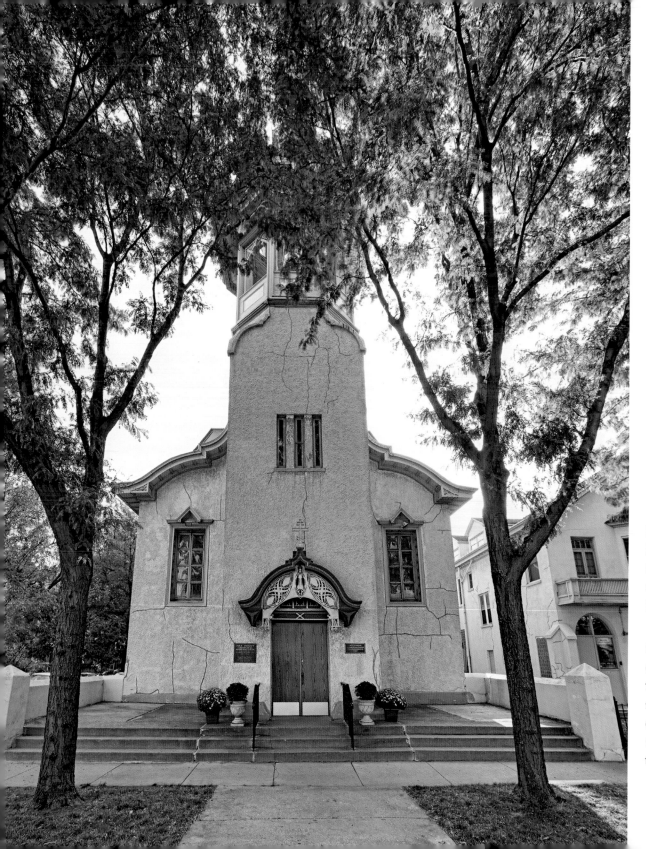

Left: One of Sullivan's most charming small buildings is the Holy Trinity Russian Orthodox Cathedral (Chicago, 1900). Its basic materials are stucco with wood trim. The segmented arch is repeated in the entry door and roof.

Opposite: This side view shows the cathedral's octagonal dome. When Sullivan took over this commission from another architect, he studied Orthodox practices and traditions and consulted with members of the congregation. His design honors traditions while bringing them up to date.

A view from the other side more clearly shows the spire with its characteristic onion finial.

The basic design and some of the decorative trim are original, but, as is common with many cathedrals, elements have been added over the years as the congregation could afford them. The iconostasis (altarpiece) was donated by Czar Nicholas II, later the victim, with his family, of the Russian Revolution of 1917.

The large sanctuary windows have eighteen panes of a simple geometric design. They contrast strongly with the elaborate decorations that surround them. The chandelier is by Louis Comfort Tiffany.

The tomb for Carrie Eliza Getty (1890) in Chicago's Graceland Cemetery (final resting place for the city's elite, including George Pullman, Marshall Field, and Sullivan himself) shows the architect's genius in miniature. Constructed of gray limestone, it is at once Romanesque and Moorish, its decorations perfectly proportioned to the size of the structure.

The tomb for Martin Ryerson, a client of Adler & Sullivan, was built after his death in 1887. Constructed of granite and blue polished limestone, the tomb has a decidedly Egyptian form. Much larger than the Getty Tomb, it is almost devoid of decoration.

DECLINE AND TRIUMPH

George Grant Elmslie was Louis Sullivan's most faithful friend, and he was clearly distressed when Sullivan's lack of commissions forced him finally to leave the firm in 1909, after twenty years of collaboration and employment. For some time Elmslie had been on half pay, with the understanding that he would inherit the firm upon Sullivan's retirement or death. But half of what was essentially nothing was not enough, so Elmslie left to begin what would be a successful partnership with William Gray Purcell.

In the five years since completion of the last of the Schlesinger & Mayer commissions in 1903, Sullivan had averaged only one completed building per year. Perhaps the most significant for his future career was the National Farmers' Bank in Owatonna, Minnesota, the first of the small-town banks that would be the highlight of his last years. The design for this bank was largely Elmslie's, but Sullivan would go on to build seven more on his own.

Elmslie also did much of the design for the now demolished Henry Babson House in Riverside, Illinois, but he made it clear in a 1936 letter to Frank Lloyd Wright that the surviving Harold C. Bradley House in Madison, Wisconsin, was largely Sullivan's own design. Although Sullivan wasn't to have Elmslie's help after the Bradley House, he would have the assistance of the young architect Parker Berry, who later died during the influenza epidemic of 1918.

In the same letter, Elmslie mentioned Sullivan's design for St. Paul's Methodist Episcopal Church in Cedar Rapids, Iowa. Sullivan's disputes with the client led to his replacement with another architect, who "made a mess of the original design." Elmslie was asked to step in "and bring back some of the original idea," which he did while refusing any payment. It was another example, Elmslie wrote, of how he "had to defend him, time and again, and pacify his clients." It was this ability, as much as Elmslie's talent, that Sullivan would miss in the years to come.

In addition to the banks, Sullivan designed a small office building and a small department store, both in Iowa. But it is the banks that are best known. Although they vary in detail, they share simple cubelike forms and elaborate decoration. They are on a

smaller scale than their big-city counterparts, but their interiors nevertheless provide the same dignity and solidity that banks were then thought to require.

In a sense, these banks and Sullivan's last commission—the façade for the Krause Music Store in Chicago—were a last hurrah for the kind of decorative design that Sullivan championed throughout his career. Architecture was moving toward a stripped-down classicism and then to a functionalism that eschewed decoration altogether. That, indeed, may be the reason Sullivan's remaining buildings are so admired and even revered.

The Babson dining room had a round table and a buffet with built-in light fixtures on the end piers. The landscape mural above the fireplace is a typical Prairie-style touch. Photograph courtesy Ryerson and Burnham Libraries, Art Institute of Chicago.

The only surviving building from the Babson estate is this three-car garage (1916), designed by Elmslie and his partner William Gray Purcell after Elmslie left Sullivan's employ. It has since been converted to a private home.

The Harold C. Bradley House (Madison, Wisconsin, 1909) was commissioned by Chicago industrialist Charles Crane for his daughter Josephine and her husband, Harold Bradley. Sullivan's first plan was rejected as too grandiose. His second attempt was accepted, although the Bradleys were never comfortable there and sold the building in 1915 to its current occupants, the Sigma Phi fraternity chapter at the University of Wisconsin. The Bradleys then commissioned Purcell and Elmslie to design a more modest home. A 1972 fire caused major damage to the Bradley House, particularly to the second floor. Alumni Arthur C. Nielsen Sr. and Arthur C. Nielsen Jr. spearheaded restoration efforts.

The plan is a modified cruciform, with a gallery providing access to the various rooms and, here, to a screened staircase leading to the bedroom level.

Another view of the gallery. The woodwork and trim are oak. The settle, although appropriate, is not original. The light fixtures are of a uniform design, whether used in sconces, in chandeliers, or atop decorative piers.

This built-in desk is in the library. The basic art glass design was used not only for windows but also for book-case and other doors.

A prominent feature of the library is a circular bay with bench seating. The grille in the center section would have hidden a radiator.

While the basic design of the Bradley House was Sullivan's, a falling-out between architect and client led Crane to bring Elmslie back (he had by then left Sullivan) to complete the interior decoration. This fireplace mosaic may be his work, but Sullivan was still employing George Healy and Louis Millet—who had collaborated with him on major projects such as the Auditorium Building and the Chicago Stock Exchange—for similar work in other commissions, so they might have been the designers.

A view of the living room, with French doors leading to the porch beyond. The chairs in the foreground are the only two remaining from the dining room and were designed by Elmslie.

Opposite: The living room fireplace is similar to the one in the library but lacks a mosaic.

The dining room continues in its original use, albeit now accommodating the twenty-odd fraternity brothers who typically live in the house. The large table, designed to seat twenty, is original. The original chairs were much more elaborate, but only two survive.

Massive steel cantilevers, encased in Elmslie-designed trim, support sleeping porches for bedrooms above. This lower porch is off the living room. The swing, while not original, is based on motifs Elmslie used in a crib design. The swing was designed by two members of the fraternity.

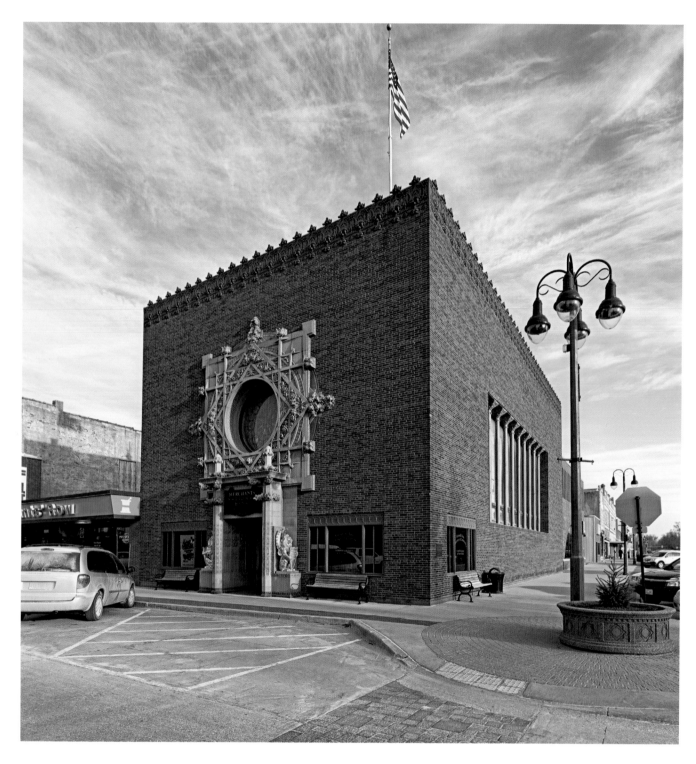

Merchants National Bank
(Grinnell, Iowa, 1914) is typical
of Sullivan's banks. Set on a
corner, its simple cubelike form
is the background for a highly
decorative main entrance.

Lovingly maintained, the bank is now the headquarters of the Grinnell Area Chamber of Commerce, the bank having moved to premises more suitable to modern banking practices.

The bank's ten art glass windows, separated by delicate columns with foliate capitals, occupy a space fifteen feet high by forty feet wide.

In this bank the windows face east. Their muted colors suit the building's conservative purpose.

The art glass skylight, whose colors emulate the sky above, provides additional natural light for the main banking hall. The clock has a mosaic surround designed by Louis Millet of Healy & Millet, a frequent Sullivan collaborator.

The rose window above the entrance, combining geometric and organic forms, is a Sullivan tour de force.

The Peoples Federal Savings and Loan Association (Sidney, Ohio, 1917) shares its basic form with Merchants National Bank. The windows are framed with elaborate terra-cotta moldings, while the cornice has a simple geometric design.

The entrance is guarded by winged lions, traditional guardians and symbols of peace. The simple word "Thrift" is surrounded by a mosaic whose cost was probably anything but thrifty.

The main banking hall is very little changed. The settle is original.

The banking hall terminates with the vault, its polished functionalism surrounded by richly carved oak woodwork. The walls and piers are Roman brick.

Abundant natural light enters the hall from west windows and an overhead skylight. Its colors, like those used in Merchants National Bank, suggest the sky above.

Opposite: A detail of one of the piers with its planter. The windows are subtly colored in shades of blue, green, and pink, with cruciform medallions in the center.

Thirsty or not, it would be hard to resist getting a drink of water from this fountain; nor were the younger customers forgotten!

The bank's conference room is paneled in the same beautifully figured quartersawn oak as used on the main banking floor. The table is original.

The Farmers and Merchants Union Bank (Columbus, Wisconsin, 1919) was Sullivan's last bank; indeed, it was his last major commission. The terra-cotta shields flanking the bank's name show the year the bank was founded, 1861, and the date the new bank was completed. Winged lions guard the entrance. The eagle at the top of the building honored the bank president's father. It symbolizes "Old Abe," mascot of the 8th Wisconsin Infantry, which fought in the Civil War.

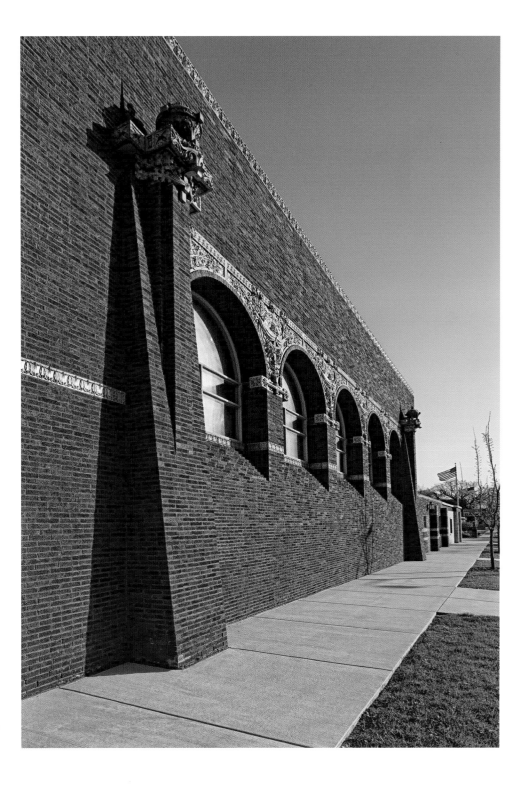

The arched windows are surrounded by terra-cotta moldings.
The flanking brick buttresses are capped by foliate capitals.

The main banking hall is relatively narrow. The red Roman brick used in the interior is brown, rather than the red flecked with blue Sullivan specified for the exterior.

The art glass windows, here viewed from a balcony above the main entrance, were executed in shades of yellow, green, and ruby red. They are among the finest Sullivan ever designed.

This arched window is just above the main entrance. It is divided into nine panes.

This window is opposite and surrounds a door leading to offices. Of the same basic design, it is divided into thirteen panes.

Opposite: Sullivan was hired to design the façade of the Krause Music Store on Lincoln Avenue in Chicago. Built in 1922, it included an owner's apartment on the second floor. While it has had many tenants over the years, it remains in good condition. Even at the end, Sullivan was incapable of doing less than his best.

Right: This elaborate medallion—with Krause's initial at its center—caps the last design one of America's greatest architects would produce. Before his death, on April 14, 1924, Sullivan would see his *Autobiography* and *System of Architectural Ornament* in print. It must have given him great satisfaction that they were published by the American Institute of Architects, which he had faithfully served for many years and which had kept him on the membership rolls even when he could no longer pay his dues.

Select Bibliography

There have been several biographies of Louis Sullivan and many studies of his work. I have listed below those that were most helpful in preparing this book. Of the biographies, the most recent, reliable, and readable is Professor Robert Twombly's *Louis Sullivan: His Life and Work*. And I would like to express my admiration for Professor Joseph Siry, whose writing on Sullivan's Auditorium and Guaranty buildings was so helpful to me. Our previous book on Frank Lloyd Wright's Unity Temple also owes much to his scholarship.

BOOKS

Condit, Carl W. *The Chicago School of Architecture: A History of Commercial and Public Building in the Chicago Area, 1875–1925*. Chicago: University of Chicago Press, 1964.

Connely, Willard. *Louis Sullivan as He Lived: The Shaping of American Architecture, a Biography*. New York: Horizon Press, 1960.

Frazier, Nancy. *Louis Sullivan and the Chicago School*. Avenel, NJ: Crescent Books, 1991.

Manieri Elia, Mario. *Louis Henry Sullivan*. New York: Princeton Architectural Press, 1996.

Morrison, Hugh. *Louis Sullivan: Prophet of Modern Architecture*. New York: Museum of Modern Art and W. W. Norton, 1935.

O'Gorman, James F. *Three American Architects: Richardson, Sullivan, and Wright, 1865–1915*. Chicago: University of Chicago Press, 1992.

Schmitt, Ronald E. *Sullivanesque: Urban Architecture and Ornamentation*. Urbana: University of Illinois Press, 2002.

Siry, Joseph M. *The Chicago Auditorium Building: Adler and Sullivan's Architecture and the City*. Chicago: University of Chicago Press, 2002.

Sullivan, Louis H. *The Autobiography of an Idea*. New York: Press of the American Institute of Architects, 1924.

———. *Kindergarten Chats and Other Writings*. New York: Dover Publications, 1979.

Szarkowski, John. *The Idea of Louis Sullivan,* new ed. Boston: Bullfinch Press, Little, Brown and Company, 2000.

Twombly, Robert C. *Louis Sullivan: His Life and Work*. Chicago: University of Chicago Press, 1987.

———, ed. *Louis Sullivan: The Public Papers*. Chicago: University of Chicago Press, 1988.

Wit, Wim de, ed. *Louis Sullivan: The Function of Ornament*. New York: W. W. Norton, 1986.

ARTICLES

Gebhard, David. "Louis Sullivan and George Grant Elmslie." *Journal of the Society of Architectural Historians* 19, no. 2 (May 1960): 62–68.

Peisch, Mark L. Letter to the editor, with letter from George G. Elmslie to Frank Lloyd Wright dated June 12, 1936, attached. *Journal of the Society of Architectural Historians* 20, no. 3 (October 1961): 140–141.

Siry, Joseph M. "Adler and Sullivan's Guaranty Building in Buffalo." *Journal of the Society of Architectural Historians* 55, no. 1 (March 1996): 6–37.

Index of Buildings

Note: Index lists photographs of Sullivan-designed buildings.